Core French

Reproducibles and Activities

Grades 4-6

By
Joanna Hourihane

Author: Joanna Hourihane

Layout Editor: Neil Hourihane

Cover Design: Berit Hansen

ISBN-13: 978-0980951400

Table of Contents

Introduction

Core French Reproducibles and Activities is a resource designed to help teachers teach beginner level French to intermediate students.

The book is arranged into eight units consisting of several thematically linked sections. The first five units also include a cumulative check-up.

Each section has a set of themed vocabulary words to focus the student learning. There are then some practice exercises to help students become more familiar with the meanings of the vocabulary words. Each section concludes with some suggested individual, group, or whole class activities to round out the learning. These activities occasionally involve internet research, using various media, or working on a homework project.

Core French Reproducibles and Activities also includes a section that suggests some supplementary activities that can be used to help add to the students' understanding of the topics covered in the book.

Unit One: Calendar

Calendar

A. Vocabulary List

janvier	_____
février	_____
mars	_____
avril	_____
mai	_____
juin	_____
juillet	_____
août	_____
septembre	_____
octobre	_____
novembre	_____
décembre	_____
lundi	_____
mardi	_____
mercredi	_____
jeudi	_____
vendredi	_____
samedi	_____
dimanche	_____
Quelle est la date?	_____

B. Translate into French.

What is the date?

_____

It is Thursday, August 5th.

_____

It is Friday, December 9th.

_____

Sunday	_____	Tuesday	_____
April	_____	Saturday	_____
November	_____	July	_____
March	_____	January	_____
Friday	_____	October	_____
December	_____	August	_____
May	_____	Monday	_____
Wednesday	_____	June	_____
February	_____	Thursday	_____

C. Use the word bank below to complete this activity.

1) What is the first month of the year? _____

2) In what month is Halloween? _____

3) What are the weekend days? _____

_____

4) What is the first **school** day of the week? _____

5) In what month is Valentine's Day? _____

6) In what month is Remembrance day? _____

7) What are the two months of summer _____

vacation? _____

8) What is the last month of the school year? _____

9) What is the first month of the school year? _____

10) In what month is Christmas? _____

11) How would you ask someone the date? _____

12) What are two months in spring? _____

_____

janvier	samedi	décembre	juillet
juin	lundi	août	février
septembre	novembre	Quelle est la date?	octobre
dimanche	mai	avril	

D. Unscramble these words.

verrife   _____   deamis   _____

menobrev   _____   niju   _____

betperesm   _____   robotec   _____

telluji   _____   auto   _____

ranvije   _____   breedemc   _____

handmice   _____   ami   _____

viral   _____   ramid   _____

drimecre   _____   ueijd   _____

drivened   _____   sarm   _____

E. Answer these questions in complete sentences.

1) Quelle est la date de ton anniversaire?

_____

2) Quelle est la date aujourd'hui (today)?

_____

3) Quelle est la date de Noël?

_____

F. Calendar

Put the blank calendar page provided into your French cahier. You will get one every month.

Your teacher may ask you to bring out your calendar page to question you on calendar words, etc. so make sure you don't lose it.

For each month, write in the days of the week, the name of the month, any holidays that take place that month, and the numbers for the days.

You may check off days as you pass them.

To find out the names of special days or holidays, look in a French/English dictionary or at an online translation site.

Draw a picture at the top that symbolizes the month to you. Colour it as well.

Note: The French calendar's week begins with Monday and ends with Sunday.

Time and Seasons

A. Vocabulary List

l'hiver _____

l'été _____

le printemps _____

l'automne _____

le jour _____

semaine _____

le moi _____

l'an _____

une seconde _____

une minute _____

une heure _____

le matin _____

le soir _____

l'après-midi _____

la nuit _____

demain _____

hier _____

aujourd'hui _____

le premier _____

la deuxième _____

la troisième _____

l'anniversaire _____

B. Translate into French.

third	_____	birthday	_____
summer	_____	week	_____
tomorrow	_____	year	_____
day	_____	autumn	_____
evening	_____	morning	_____
second	_____	hour	_____
month	_____	winter	_____
first	_____	night	_____
afternoon	_____	today	_____
yesterday	_____	spring	_____
minute	_____	second	_____

C. Use the word bank below to complete this activity.

1) What are the four seasons?   _____

_____   _____   _____

2) If today is Wednesday, then what was Tuesday?   _____

3) If today is Wednesday, then what is Thursday?   _____

4) If you were born on this date, it is what?   _____

5) February is one of these.   _____

6) Usually, you wake up at this time of day.   _____

7) Most people are asleep at this time.   _____

8) Seven days.   _____

9) Twenty-four hours.   _____

10) Sixty seconds.   _____

11) If you win a race, you came in what place?   _____

12) Sixty minutes.   _____

13) This day.   _____

le jour	l'automne	une semaine	un jour
le premier	l'hiver	l'été	hier
la nuit	le printemps	l'anniversaire	une minute
demain	le matin	une heure	aujourd'hui
un moi	l'an	le soir	l'après-midi

D. Mots Cachés

```
A  S  P  M  E  T  N  I  R  P  E  L
U  P  E  W  R  Z  H  D  G  M  M  E
J  R  T  M  I  I  A  E  E  C  A  M
O  E  U  Q  A  T  D  I  U  P  A  E
U  M  N  C  S  I  X  Z  R  R  R  I
R  I  I  H  R  U  N  E  S  E  E  S
D  E  M  C  E  N  S  E  V  T  H  I
H  R  O  D  V  M  C  I  E  Q  I  O
U  I  B  J  I  O  H  M  O  I  E  R
I  L  O  D  N  I  A  M  E  D  R  T
Y  U  I  D  N  A  U  T  O  M  N  E
R  E  E  M  A  T  I  N  R  I  O  S
```

ANNIVERSAIRE	APRÈS-MIDI	AUJOURD'HUI
AUTOMNE	DEMAIN	DEUXIÈME
ÉTÉ	HEURE	HIER
HIVER	JOUR	MATIN
MINUTE	MOI	NUIT
PREMIER	PRINTEMPS	SECONDE
SEMAINE	SOIR	TROISIÈME

Weather

A. Vocabulary List

Quel temps fait-il? _____

Il neige. _____

Il pleut. _____

Il fait du soleil. _____

Il fait beau. _____

Il fait mauvais. _____

Il fait froid. _____

Il fait chaud. _____

Il fait du brouillard. _____

Il fait du vent. _____

Il fait nuageux. _____

Il fait frais. _____

Notice that in French we don't use "ÊTRE" or say that the weather "IS" a certain way. We always use the verb "FAIRE".

B. Translate into French.

How's the weather? _____

It's nice. _____

It's snowing. _____

It's sunny. _____

It's hot. _____

It's raining. _____

It's cool. _____

It's foggy. _____

It's not nice. _____

It's windy. _____

It's cloudy. _____

C. Mini-Poster Project

Create an information poster showing kinds of weather and the French sentence describing that kind of weather. Your poster should be colourful, easy to understand, neat, and detailed. Make sure you check your spelling and go over your sentences with a fine point marker or pen.

D. Mini-Charades

Act out a certain kind of weather. For example, pretend to put on some mittens and start making a snowman. Then ask "Quel temps fait-il?" The first person to give the correct answer "Il neige." gets to go next.

E. Website Activity

Go to the website for Environment Canada.	www.ec.gc.ca

Select "Français".

Select "Conditions Actuelles" to find weather forecasts.

Explore the forecasts for your region as well as other regions in Canada.

Write down five French terms in the forecasts that are unfamiliar to you and click on the "English" button to find out the English translation. Write down the translated word.

	French term	English translation
1.		
2.		
3.		
4.		
5.		

Unit One Check-Up

A. Match the French term with the English translation.

A	jeudi	_____	hot
B	dimanche	_____	night
C	la semaine	_____	spring
D	soleil	_____	Thursday
E	une heure	_____	snow
F	août	_____	winter
G	le printemps	_____	week
H	samedi	_____	Sunday
I	février	_____	hour
J	le temps	_____	weather
K	neige	_____	Saturday
L	chaud	_____	Tuesday
M	mardi	_____	cold
N	le premier	_____	sun
O	l'hiver	_____	first
P	la nuit	_____	August
Q	froid	_____	February

B. Translate the following sentences from French to English.

1. Quelle est la date?

_____

2. Il fait du soleil.

_____

3. Il fait du vent.

_____

C. Translate the following sentences from English to French.

1. It is snowing.

_____

2. It is Thursday, November 10th.

_____

Unit Two: Descriptions

Colours

A. Vocabulary List

la couleur   _____

blanc   _____

vert   _____

orange   _____

violet   _____

argent   _____

gris   _____

clair   _____

noir   _____

bleu   _____

jaune   _____

rouge   _____

brun   _____

or   _____

rose   _____

foncé   _____

Quelle couleur?   _____

B. Translate into French.

What colour is it?

_____

It is dark blue.

_____

grey	_____	gold	_____
dark	_____	orange	_____
blue	_____	red	_____
colour	_____	white	_____
green	_____	light (colour)	_____
silver	_____	black	_____
yellow	_____	brown	_____
pink	_____	purple	_____

C. Directions for making Fortune Tellers

Use the instructions below to make an origami fortune teller

Start with a square piece of paper.

Fold the square corner to corner and then do so again to make an "X".

Fold up all four corners so that the points almost meet in the middle.

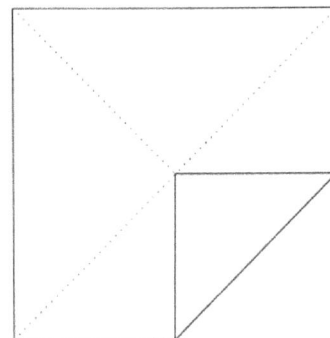

It should now look like this.

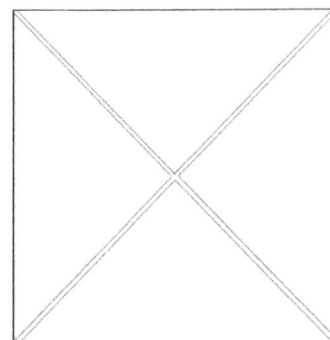

Flip it over. Fold up all four corners so the points almost meet in the middle.

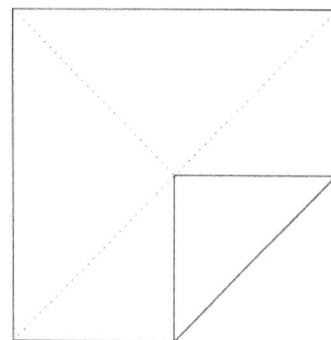

It should now look like this.

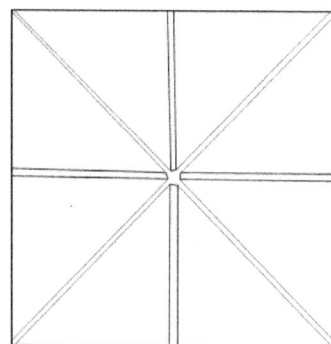

Now fold it in half with the triangles inward.

Work your fingers into the four corners from the fold side and form four points.

Label the outside squares and inside triangles as different French colours and numbers for players to choose from. Write funny and classroom-appropriate fortunes on the innermost triangles. Play fortune-telling in French!

Descriptive Words

A. Vocabulary List

grand   _____

gros   _____

beau   _____

droit   _____

vite   _____

lourd   _____

petit   _____

maigre   _____

belle   _____

vieux   _____

court   _____

nouveau   _____

rond   _____

lent   _____

léger   _____

jeune   _____

long   _____

beaucoup   _____

B. Translate into French.

It is fast.

_____

She is beautiful.

_____

long	_____	slow	_____
handsome	_____	fast	_____
new	_____	beautiful	_____
old	_____	small	_____
thin	_____	short	_____
round	_____	light	_____
big	_____	many	_____
heavy	_____	fat	_____
young	_____	straight	_____

C. Use the word bank below to complete this activity.

1) Opposite of long. _____

2) Opposite of small. _____

3) Opposite of slow. _____

4) Opposite of short. _____

5) Opposite of big. _____

6) Opposite of fast. _____

7) Opposite of heavy. _____

8) Opposite of light. _____

9) Opposite of curvy. _____

10) Opposite of bad. _____

11) Opposite of old. _____

12) Opposite of few. _____

13) Opposite of young. _____

14) Opposite of used. _____

vite	nouveau	lent
jeune	léger	court
vieux	long	grand
droit	petit	lourd
bon	beaucoup	

D. Create a Picture Book

Create a children's picture book showing the meaning of at least 10 of the words from the Vocabulary List. You can illustrate some opposites on the same page. Follow the instructions below to create your book with one piece of paper.

Directions:

Fold a letter-size piece of paper in half.

Fold that rectangle in half.

Cut through the top two folds to free all the pages for turning.

Illustrate the title page. Make your own title. (E.g. "Les Opposites" or "Les Descriptions")

Illustrate and label your book pages.

E. Sharing Your Book

Visit a younger class or your buddy class and share your book with a younger student. See if you can teach a couple of French words to a young child.

Numbers

A. Vocabulary List

zéro _____

un _____

deux _____

trois _____

quatre _____

cinq _____

six _____

sept _____

huit _____

neuf _____

dix _____

onze _____

douze _____

treize _____

quatorze _____

quinze _____

seize _____

dix-sept _____

dix-huit _____

dix-neuf _____

vingt _____

vingt-et-un _____

trente _____

quarante _____

cinquante _____

soixante _____

soixante-dix _____

quatre-vingt _____

quatre-vingt-dix _____

cent _____

Combien? _____

B. Translate into French.

forty	_____	thirteen	_____
seven	_____	ninety	_____
four	_____	one hundred	_____
fifty	_____	eighty	_____
twenty-one	_____	twelve	_____
fourteen	_____	sixty	_____
five	_____	eleven	_____
seventy	_____	twenty	_____
eight	_____	three	_____
thirty	_____	nineteen	_____
sixteen	_____	eighteen	_____

C. Play Number Toss

Use a soft or sponge ball for this game.

The whole class or a group of students can play in one game.

The person who starts says "zero" and tosses the ball gently to another student. That student says "un" and passes to someone else, who says "deux". The ball continues to be passed until someone drops the ball or makes an error in counting.

To make it more challenging, students can skip count (count by 2's or 5's).

D. Play Number Game

The class is divided into 2 teams and each team lines up on opposite sides of the gym.

Each student "counts off" or is assigned a number (like from 1 to 15) in French.

The teacher puts an object in the centre of the gym.

The teacher calls out a number (in French or English) and that student from each team races to get the object first.

To make this more challenging, the teacher could call out equations. For example, the students assigned the number "sept" would run to the middle when they figure out the answer for "trois plus quatre".

E. Play "Phone Numbers"

Each student should write down their phone number in numerals (e.g. 555-2323) on a piece of paper.

Collect the phone numbers and hand them back out randomly.

Each student reads out the phone number that they received and the corresponding student may be seated.

Keep going until all students are seated.

F. Play "BEEP"

Students stand in a line or in a circle.

They then begin to "count off" by ones.

Whenever a number which includes a "4" comes up, the student whose turn it is must say "BEEP" instead of the number. For example, "BEEP" would replace 4, 14, 24, 34, 40-49, 54, etc.

See how high the class can count.

The "BEEP" number can be changed to something else after a few tries.

Unit Two Check-Up

A. Match the French term with the English translation.

A	gris	_____	fifteen
B	rose	_____	yellow
C	soixante	_____	fat
D	jaune	_____	grey
E	vieux	_____	fast
F	vingt	_____	beautiful
G	blanc	_____	forty
H	treize	_____	black
I	quarante	_____	eleven
J	gros	_____	five
K	noir	_____	old
L	vite	_____	young
M	onze	_____	many
N	quinze	_____	twenty
O	jeune	_____	white
P	belle	_____	pink
Q	beaucoup	_____	thirteen
R	cinq	_____	yellow

B. Translate the following sentences from French to English.

1. C'est noir.   _____

2. C'est grand.   _____

C. Translate the following sentences from English to French.

1. How many?

_____

2. It is light green.

_____

D. Write the numbers (e.g. trois = 3)

cinquante   _____   douze   _____

cent   _____   dix-sept   _____

huit   _____   soixante-dix   _____

onze   _____   quatre-vingt   _____

quinze   _____   deux   _____

Unit Three:
Objects

Articles

A. Vocabulary List

le	l'	un	des
la	les	une	

B. Important Concepts

In French we use articles in naming objects more often than in English.

In French, objects are always either masculine or feminine and the correct article must be chosen.

There are also articles demonstrating that there is more than one of an object.

THE	A
le (masculine)	**un** (masculine)
la (feminine)	**une** (feminine)
l' (when the object starts with a vowel)	*
les (plural)	**des** (plural)

Always using an article with the name of the object will help you remember whether objects are masculine or feminine.

The Classroom

A. Vocabulary List

le livre   _____

le crayon   _____

la gomme   _____

la poubelle   _____

l'étudiant   _____

l'instructeur   _____

la craie   _____

le cahier   _____

le stylo   _____

le pupitre   _____

l'ordinateur   _____

le bureau   _____

le tableau   _____

le papier   _____

une salle de classe   _____

un sac à dos   _____

la brosse   _____

la porte   _____

une école   _____

la règle   _____

bibliothèque   _____

la chaise   _____

B. Translate into French. Include the article.

ruler	_____	trash can	_____
teacher	_____	teacher desk	_____
computer	_____	student desk	_____
notebook	_____	chalkboard	_____
textbook	_____	backpack	_____
chalk	_____	pen	_____
student	_____	school	_____
paper	_____	classroom	_____
brush	_____	window	_____
door	_____	chair	_____
library	_____	eraser	_____

C. Use the word bank below to complete this activity.

1) What do you use to erase mistakes? _____

2) When at school, a student sits at this. _____

3) Throw garbage in this. _____

4) You write on this with chalk. _____

5) A school is full of this kind of room. _____

6) This has a screen and a keyboard. _____

7) Use this to do math so you can erase your mistakes. _____

8) Use this to carry your books to school. _____

9) Measure things with this. _____

10) A kid in school is called this. _____

11) You write notes in this kind of book. _____

12) You can borrow books here. _____

13) You use this to write on a blackboard. _____

un étudiant	la salle de classe	la bibliothèque
la craie	la poubelle	une gomme
un pupitre	le tableau	un cahier
un sac a dos	une règle	un ordinateur
un crayon		

D. Play Quick Draw

The class is divided into two teams.

The teacher has a set of cue cards with classroom objects on them.

The teacher shows a card to one person from each team and they draw the object on the board (or on individual chart paper) for their team.

The first team to say the object correctly in French gets a point.

E. Play Hangman

The teacher has a list ready of classroom object vocabulary or questions pertaining to classroom vocabulary.

The class is divided into two teams.

The teacher or a student can be the hangman. The hangman should draw two empty gallows on the board, one for each team.

Directions

The first player from each team goes to different ends of the same chalkboard or different chart paper.

The teacher asks a question or reads a vocabulary word. The two students write their answers without help from their team mates.

The teacher checks the answers and instructs the hangman to add a body part to the gallows for any incorrect answer.

The game continues until one of the teams has a complete person hanging.

Home

A. Vocabulary List

la maison   _____

la salle   _____

la porte   _____

la fenêtre   _____

la salle de bain   _____

la cuisine   _____

le lit   _____

le téléphone   _____

la télévision   _____

la voiture   _____

le jardin   _____

la bicyclette   _____

la table   _____

la chaise   _____

le réfrigérateur   _____

la lumière   _____

la chambre   _____

le plancher   _____

le mur   _____

le plafond   _____

le toît   _____

B. Translate into French

It is a car.

_____

It is a bicycle.

_____

kitchen _____   bedroom _____

bed _____   house _____

door· _____   television _____

yard _____   light _____

chair _____   window _____

room _____   roof _____

car _____   telephone _____

bicycle _____   table _____

bathroom _____   fridge _____

ceiling _____   floor _____

wall _____

C. Use the word bank below to complete this activity.

1) Where do you take a bath? _____

2) This is made of glass. _____

3) You enter and exit a room through this. _____

4) Call someone on this. _____

5) You watch shows on this. _____

6) You sit on this. _____

7) You cook supper in this room. _____

8) This is a motor vehicle. _____

9) Keep food cold here. _____

10) You sleep on this. _____

11) Your house's grass and gardens are located here. _____

12) You sleep in this room. _____

une chambre	une voiture	le jardin
la porte	la cuisine	la salle de bain
le réfrigérateur	la téléphone	un lit
une chaise	la fenêtre	la télévision

D. House Diagram

Draw a diagram of a house, labeling all of the objects and places on your **Vocabulary List**.

Write clearly and go over your printing with a fine point marker or pen afterwards.

Colour your diagram and add interesting details.

E. Model House

Materials: shoebox

fabrics, string, yarn, construction paper, cardboard, etc

colours and paints

Bring a shoebox or other similar box to school. Decorate the inside with any materials your teacher provides.

Create furniture and other household goods using cardboard and other materials.

Label at least 10 of the objects from your **Home Vocabulary List** on your model.

F. Create a Word Search

Create your own Word Search using the paper provided by your teacher. Include all the **Vocabulary List** words for this section.

When you are done, hand it in. Your teacher will redistribute them and a classmate can complete your puzzle.

Food

A. Vocabulary List

manger   _____

la nourriture   _____

le sucre   _____

le beurre   _____

le pain   _____

le sandwich   _____

le fromage   _____

la viande   _____

la pomme   _____

la banane   _____

l'orange   _____

la pomme de terre   _____

la carotte   _____

le boisson   _____

de l'eau   _____

du lait   _____

du café   _____

le jus   _____

du thé   _____

le déjeuner   _____

le dîner   _____

le souper   _____

B. Translate into French

I eat breakfast. _____

I eat the apple. _____

breakfast	_____	water	_____
eat	_____	tea	_____
apple	_____	sugar	_____
food	_____	bread	_____
supper	_____	potato	_____
coffee	_____	milk	_____
lunch	_____	sandwich	_____
banana	_____	juice	_____
orange	_____	cheese	_____
meat	_____	drink	_____
carrot	_____	butter	_____

C. Use the word bank below to complete this activity.

1) This can be white or whole wheat. _____

2) This is grown underground. _____

3) Name 3 fruits. _____

_____

_____

4) Name 3 meals. _____

_____

_____

5) Name 2 hot drinks. _____

_____

6) Name 3 cold drinks. _____

_____

_____

7) This has milk as an ingredient. _____

de l'eau	le fromage	le dîner
du café	du jus	la pomme
le souper	la banane	le pain
la pomme de terre	l'orange	du thé
du lait	le déjeuner	la banane

D. Homework Project

In Canada, manufacturers of food need to put both English and French language on packaging.

Go home and look at food packaging in your cupboards and refrigerator.

List the names of at least 10 kinds of foods that aren't on your Vocabulary List.

Also, by looking at packages at home, find the French translations for these English terms.

nutrition _____   iron   _____

calories _____   ingredient _____

fat   _____   mineral   _____

vitamin _____

Nature

A. Vocabulary List

le monde   _____

la montagne   _____

l'océan   _____

l'arbre   _____

la roche   _____

la terre   _____

la rivière   _____

le lac   _____

la fleur   _____

le parc   _____

l'animal   _____

le chien   _____

le chat   _____

le poisson   _____

le cheval   _____

la poule   _____

l'ours   _____

la vache   _____

le cochon   _____

l'oiseau   _____

la souris   _____

B. Translate into French

fish	_____	bear	_____
land	_____	park	_____
bird	_____	animal	_____
world	_____	dog	_____
rock	_____	cat	_____
cow	_____	river	_____
mountain	_____	horse	_____
ocean	_____	cow	_____
pig	_____	flower	_____
lake	_____	chicken	_____
mouse	_____	tree	_____

It is a tree.

C. Use the word bank below to complete this activity.

1) This is made of petals and a stem. _____

2) This is able to fly. _____

3) "Pacific" is the name of one of these. _____

4) Bacon is made from this animal. _____

5) A playground is often found here. _____

6) Beef comes from this animal. _____

7) A salmon is a kind of what? _____

8) What kind of animal barks? _____

9) What kind of animal meows? _____

10) This is the name of our planet. _____

11) This kind of bird does not fly. _____

12) Everest is an example of one of these landforms. _____

un chat	une fleur	une poule
une montagne	un parc	un oiseau
une vache	un poisson	un océan
un cochon	un chien	la Terre

D. Play Quick Draw

The class is divided into two teams.

The teacher has a set of cue cards with nature and animal terms on them.

The teacher shows a card to one person from each team and they draw the object or animal on the board (or on individual chart paper) for their team.

The first team to say the answer correctly in French gets a point.

E. Play Vocabulary Charades

The class is divided into two teams.

The teacher has a set of cue cards with nature and animal terms on them.

The teacher shows one member of a team the card and that team member has one minute to act out what is written on the card.

Nothing can be said by the person and no clues about spelling (e.g. what letter the term begins with) can be given.

The team gets a point for a correct answer in French.

The teams continue to alternate turns until a set number of turns (usually until everyone gets a turn).

Unit 3 Check-Up

A. Match the French term with the English.

A	le cahier	_____	bird
B	le déjeuner	_____	computer
C	le fromage	_____	pen
D	la chambre	_____	bread
E	la chaise	_____	bed
F	l'ordinateur	_____	cheese
G	le stylo	_____	desk
H	l'oiseau	_____	notebook
I	la vache	_____	chair
J	la fenêtre	_____	dog
K	le pain	_____	food
L	le lit	_____	breakfast
M	le poisson	_____	window
N	le chien	_____	fish
O	le pupitre	_____	bedroom
P	la nourriture	_____	cow

B. Translate the following sentences from French to English.

1. C'est une maison.

_____

2. C'est une fleur.

_____

C. Translate the following sentences from English to French.

1. It is a pencil. _____

2. It is a cat. _____

D. Choose le, la, or les.

_____ papier   _____ école

_____ ordinateur   _____ pomme

Unit Four:
Language

Pronouns

A. Vocabulary List

je   _____   nous   _____

tu   _____   vous   _____

il   _____   ils   _____

elle   _____   elles   _____

B. Translate into French.

she   _____   you (1 person)   _____

he   _____   they (girls)   _____

I   _____   you (2 people)   _____

we   _____   they (boys)   _____

C. Draw a picture to show what these pronouns mean.

Il	Je	Elles

Avoir

A. Vocabulary List

J'ai   _____   Nous avons   _____

Tu as   _____   Vous avez   _____

Il a   _____   Ils ont   _____

Elle a   _____   Elles ont   _____

B. Translate into French.

She has   _____   They have (3 boys)   _____

We have   _____   You have (one person)   _____

I have   _____   They have (3 girls)   _____

He has   _____   You have (2 people)   _____

C. Practice Time

Recite the Vocabulary List for **Avoir** until you have it memorized.

Then find a partner and test each other.

Try to write all the pronouns and forms of **Avoir** that go with them without looking at your list.

Être

A. Vocabulary List

Je suis _____   Nous sommes _____

Tu es _____   Vous êtes _____

Il est _____   Ils sont _____

Elle est _____   Elles sont _____

B. Translate into French

You are _____   We are _____
(2 people)

They are _____   He is _____
 (4 girls)

You are _____   I am _____
(1 person)

They are _____   She is _____
(4 boys)

C. Practice Time

Recite the Vocabulary List for **Être** until you have it memorized.

Then find a partner and test each other.

Try to write all the pronouns and forms of **Être** that go with them without looking at your list.

Actions

A. Vocabulary Words

il mange _____

elle chante _____

il parle _____

elle ouvre _____

il regarde _____

elle joue _____

il aime _____

elle tombe _____

elle pense _____

il écrit _____

elle lit _____

il ferme _____

elle travaille _____

il saute _____

elle écoute _____

il marche _____

B. Translate into French

He eats an apple.

_____

She likes the dog.

_____

he walks	_____	she jumps	_____
she eats	_____	he looks	_____
he falls	_____	she likes	_____
she works	_____	he closes	_____
he talks	_____	she opens	_____
she writes	_____	he sings	_____
he plays	_____	she hears	_____
she thinks	_____	he reads	_____

C. Research what the infinitive form of the verb is.

For example: *"he eats" = to eat*

"il mange = manger"

il chante _____   il tombe _____

il travaille _____   il marche _____

il parle _____   il ouvre _____

il regarde _____   il jour _____

il aime _____   il mange _____

il saute _____   il écoute _____

il écrit _____   il pense _____

il ferme _____   il lit _____

D. Create a word scramble or word search

Use the words above (the infinitive, "full" forms of the verbs) in a word search or in a word scramble. Hand these in.

E. Play Charades

Take turns acting out one of the Vocabulary List words and having your friends guess what you are doing.

They must guess in French!

This game may be played in teams as well.

Try doing other vocabulary words you've learned as well so it's harder for everyone to guess what you might be acting out.

F. Play "Simon Dit"

This is the same as the English game "Simon Says".

The teacher or a student is the leader, "Simon".

They will give an order to do an action using the words "Simon dit…"

All students need to immediately act out the action or they are eliminated.

Also, if they start doing the action without the leader saying "Simon dit" then they are eliminated.

Emotions

A. Vocabulary List

(féminin)

Je suis content. _____ contente

Je suis excité _____ excité

Je suis triste. _____

Je suis solitaire. _____

Je suis gentil. _____ gentille

Je suis courageux. _____ courageuse

Je suis fâché. _____ fâchée

Je suis tranquille. _____

Je suis fatigué. _____ fatiguée

Je suis nerveux. _____ nerveuse

Je suis timide. _____

Je suis fier. _____ fière

Je suis curieux. _____ curieuse

Je suis jaloux. _____ jalouse

Je suis déçu. _____ déçue

J'ai faim. _____

J'ai peur. _____

B. Translate into French.

I am sad.

_____

I am hungry.

_____

I'm disappointed.

_____

brave	_____	calm	_____
happy	_____	hungry	_____
lonely	_____	timid	_____
anxious	_____	tired	_____
excited	_____	scared	_____
nice	_____	angry	_____
sad	_____	jealous	_____
curious	_____	proud	_____

C. Translate into English.

1) Elle est tranquille. _____

2) Elle est courageuse. _____

3) Elle est solitaire. _____

4) Elle a peur. _____

5) Elle est contente. _____

6) Elle est triste. _____

7) Je suis fatigué. _____

8) Nous sommes excités. _____

D. Translate into French.

1) He is tired. _____

2) He is proud. _____

3) He is nervous. _____

4) I am angry. _____

5) We are calm. _____

6) He is hungry. _____

E. Draw faces that express the emotion.

content	triste	fâché
peur	excité	tranquille
fatigué	gentil	déçu

Unit Four Check-Up

A. Match the French word with the English translation.

A	Nous avons.	_____	She is calm.
B	Ils sont.	_____	We have.
C	Elle est fâchée.	_____	She is angry.
D	Je suis content.	_____	You are sad.
E	Il chante.	_____	They are.
F	Il parle.	_____	He is tired.
G	Il mange.	_____	I am.
H	Tu es triste.	_____	He sings.
I	Je suis.	_____	I am happy.
J	Ils ont peur.	_____	They are scared.
K	Elle tombe.	_____	She falls.
L	Il est fatigué.	_____	He talks.
M	Elle est tranquille.	_____	He eats.

B. Translate the following sentences from French to English.

1) Il est excité. _____

2) J'ai faim. _____

3) Il marche à l'école. _____

4) Il aime le soleil. _____

5) Elle pense. _____

6) Il lit le livre. _____

C. Translate the following sentences from English to French.

1) She eats. _____

2) He sings. _____

3) I am. _____

4) He is. _____

5) I have. _____

Unit Five:
People

Family

A. Vocabulary List

mère   _____

soeur   _____

grand-mère   _____

le fils   _____

le bébé   _____

le garçon   _____

père   _____

frère   _____

grand-père   _____

la fille   _____

l'enfant   _____

la fille   _____

l'homme   _____

la femme   _____

la tante   _____

l'oncle   _____

le cousin   _____

le neveu   _____

la nièce   _____

l'ami   _____

B. Translate into French.

It is a baby.

_____

She is my mother.

_____

man	_____	girl	_____
mother	_____	cousin	_____
grandfather	_____	uncle	_____
friend	_____	child	_____
brother	_____	baby	_____
aunt	_____	sister	_____
father	_____	woman	_____
boy	_____	son	_____
grandmother	_____	aunt	_____
nephew	_____	niece	_____

C. Use the word band below to complete this activity.

1) These are your parents.

_____

_____

2) These are your parents'   _____

parents.

_____

3) A male adult.   _____

4) Not yet an adult.   _____

5) Not yet a child.   _____

6) A female child.   _____

7) A female adult.   _____

8) A male child.   _____

9) Your mother's sister is   _____
your…

10) This person is not related to   _____
you.

11) Your mother's brother is   _____
your…

grand-père	un homme	oncle
un enfant	grand-mère	un bébé
un ami	un garçon	mère
père	tante	une fille
une femme		

D. Create a Family Tree

Discuss family trees as a class.

Which relatives should be included and how should the branches of family member be organized?

Create your own mini-poster of your family tree. It's a good idea to do a rough draft on paper first.

Your tree should have the names of your family members as well as what relation they are to you.

Be sure to get help from your parents or grandparents if you aren't sure about some names of your relatives.

Have fun and earn extra point on this assignment by making your family tree look like a tree! It should also be well-organized and neat.

Body

A. Vocabulary List

le corps _____

la tête _____

les cheveux _____

le visage _____

les yeux _____

le nez _____

la bouche _____

les oreilles _____

les dents _____

le cou _____

l'épaule _____

le bras _____

la main _____

le doigt _____

la jambe _____

le genou _____

le pied _____

l'estomac _____

la derrière _____

le dos _____

B. Translate into French.

back _____ face _____

hand _____ body _____

stomach _____ ears _____

nose _____ head _____

mouth _____ leg _____

behind (bum) _____ foot _____

eyes _____ arm _____

finger _____ neck _____

hair _____ teeth _____

shoulder _____ knee _____

I have brown hair.

_____

She has white teeth.

_____

C. Use the word bank below to complete this activity.

1) This gets stuffed up when you
have a cold.   _____

2) Tears come out of these.   _____

3) You bite with these.   _____

4) You point with this.   _____

5) You give a "high-five" with this.   _____

6) You comb this.   _____

7) Your tongue is in here.   _____

8) Your belly button is here.   _____

9) You listen with these.   _____

10) Your hair grows on this.   _____

11) Your shoes go on these.   _____

les yeux	le doigt	les cheveux
les pieds	l'estomac	la tête
les dents	la bouche	le nez
la main	les oreilles	

D. Magazine Project

Materials: Old magazines (O.K. to cut up)

White paper (11 x 17)

Glue and a pen

For this project you will create a character by cutting parts of bodies out of magazine pictures.

Glue the body parts onto a piece of paper to make a complete new character.

Label the body parts of your character in French.

Make your character comical if you can. Labelling should be neat. You can label more parts than just those on the Vocabulary List if you choose.

E. Play "Simon Dit"

This is the same as the English game "Simon Says".

The teacher or a student is "Simon".

They instruct the class to touch body parts using the words "Simon dit".

e.g.   "Simon dit… touche la bouche."

"Simon dit… touche les pieds."

The class must follow directions quickly or they are "out" and sit down.

The class also must be careful not to follow the directions if the words "Simon dit" are not used. If they make this mistake they are "out" as well.

Clothing

A. Vocabulary List

les vêtements   _____

la chemise   _____

le chandail   _____

le T-shirt   _____

les pantalons   _____

le jean   _____

le short   _____

la robe   _____

la jupe   _____

les sous-vêtements   _____

les chaussettes   _____

les souliers   _____

les bottes   _____

le manteau   _____

le chapeau   _____

les gants   _____

les lunettes   _____

les bijoux   _____

B. Translate into French.

It is a hat.

_____

It is a coat.

_____

shoes	_____	underwear	_____
T-shirt	_____	clothing	_____
shorts	_____	pants	_____
jeans	_____	coat	_____
hat	_____	glasses	_____
shirt	_____	boots	_____
socks	_____	gloves	_____
skirt	_____	dress	_____
jewelry	_____		

C. Use the word bank below to complete this activity.

1) You wear these under your shoes.

_____

2) You wear this on top of your head.

_____

3) Wear these on your feet in rainy weather.

_____

4) Wear this instead of pants on a hot day.

_____

5) You wear these under your clothes.

_____

6) Wear these to improve your vision.

_____

7) These kinds of pants are usually blue.

_____

8) Wear this over your shirt to keep warm.

_____

9) Wear these to keep your hands warm.

_____

le jean	les bottes	le chapeau
les chaussettes	le manteau	les lunettes
les sous-vêtements	le short	les gants

D. Draw the following.

la chemise	les pantalons	les souliers
le manteau	les chaussettes	le chapeau

E. Elimination Game

The teacher calls out a colour and an article of clothing most students are wearing.

Students stand up if they are wearing a piece of clothing identified.

The last person or few people sitting win.

F. Create a Clothing Catalogue.

Create a catalogue of clothing for "sale".

You can make the catalogue for girls, boys, sportswear, or any other specialty clothing line.

Use at least 10 of the **Vocabulary List** words. You may look up other specific vocabulary if you'd like (e.g. "hockey jersey").

G. Play Identifying Game

The teacher or students bring in or contribute articles of clothing. Barbie and doll clothes are great.

Two teams are numbered off.

The teacher says a clothing term in French (e.g. chemise) and then a number.

The two students of that number race to get the article of clothing identified. If they grab it at the same time it is a tie (no tearing!).

H. Can You Find What Is Different?

A volunteer leaves the classroom.

While the volunteer is out of the room, the other students can change sweaters, coats, etc.

The student who left then returns to the classroom.

He/she has to guess which articles do not belong on the people wearing them (in French).

Unit Five Check-Up

A. Match the French term with the English translation.

A	les oreilles	_____	underwear
B	les dents	_____	arm
C	le chapeau	_____	teeth
D	la sœur	_____	eyes
E	les chaussettes	_____	shoes
F	les sous-vêtements	_____	hand
G	les yeux	_____	hair
H	le bras	_____	sister
I	la chemise	_____	boy
J	les souliers	_____	ears
K	la main	_____	shirt
L	les cheveux	_____	foot
M	le pied	_____	hat
N	le garçon	_____	socks

B. Translate the following sentences to English.

1) C'est une fille.

_____

2) C'est un chapeau.

_____

C. Draw the following.

les yeux	les lunettes	les pantalons
la bouche	les bottes	la fille

Unit Six: Conversation

Conversation

A. Vocabulary List

Bonjour   _____

Salut   _____

Bienvenue   _____

Au revoir   _____

Comment ça va?   _____

Bien   _____

Très bien   _____

Ça va   _____

Pas mal   _____

S'il vous plait _____

Excusez-moi   _____

Merci beaucoup   _____

De rien   _____

Comment t'appelles-tu? _____

Je m'appelle…   _____

Quel âge as-tu? _____

Je t'aime.   _____

Oui / Non   _____ / _____

B. Translate into French.

My name is… _____

Hi _____

O.K. _____

I love you. _____

Well. _____

Good-bye. _____

Please. _____

You're welcome. _____

Not bad. _____

Very well. _____

How are you? _____

Hello. _____

Excuse me. _____

Thank-you very much. _____

Welcome. _____

How old are you? _____

What's your name? _____

C. Use the word bank below to complete this activity.

1) This is how you introduce yourself. _____

2) This is how you ask how someone is doing. _____

3) This is how you tell someone you like them a lot. _____

4) When you leave, you say this. _____

5) You say this when you receive a gift from someone. _____

6) When someone thanks you, you can say this. _____

7) If you want something from someone, say this. _____

8) If you need to interrupt a conversation, say this. _____

9) Give two examples of greeting words. _____

_____

10) If you just won the lottery and someone asks how you are doing, you'll say this. _____

Je t'aime	Merci beaucoup.	Très bien!
Salut.	Je m'appelle	Excusez-moi.
Comment ça va?	S'il vous plait.	Bonjour.
Au revoir.	De rien.	

D. Write a Conversation

Write a conversation between two people in English.

The conversation should consist of at least 8 speaking lines.

Translate this conversation into French. You should use some of the **Vocabulary List** words and could also use other French terms. You may use an internet translation site or a French-English dictionary.

Hand in your English and French conversations. Make sure they are neat enough for the teacher to follow.

E. Role-play a Conversation

With a partner, read through the conversations you each created.

Choose one to present to the class.

If you like parts of each you may take parts of each conversation and put them together in a single presentation.

Practise and try to memorize the line.

Present it to the class.

F. What's Your Name?

A student sits at the front of the classroom with his or her back to the class.

The teacher points to students in the class and asks "Comment t'appelles-tu?"

That student must respond "Je m'appelle_____" with either their real name or the name of someone else in the class.

The teacher asks the student at the front "C'est _____?" and the student answers "Oui" or "Non".

If the student at the front is right, they continue to be at the front. If they're wrong, then they change places with the student who fooled them. To make the game more difficult and amusing, students may disguise their voices.

G. Conversation Balls

Materials: three different coloured balls (small and lightweight)

The class makes a circle.

Give three people a ball.

Blue Ball = Très bien.

Yellow Ball = Comment ça va?

Red Ball = Merci beaucoup.

The class gently passes the balls and the person who catches them says the meaning of the balls.

Questions

A. Vocabulary List

Qu'est-ce que c'est?

Combien?

Où?

Pourquoi?

Quel?

Qui?

Quand?

Comment?

Quoi?

Parce que …

C'est…

B. Translate into French.

Because	_____	Who?	_____
What is it?	_____	It is …	_____
Where?	_____	How many?	_____
What?	_____	When?	_____
How?	_____	Why?	_____
Which?	_____		

Prepositions

A. Vocabulary List

à   après

devant   avec

avant   dans

chez   derrière

de   sans

pour   sous

sur   à cote de

B. Translate into French.

in   _____   under   _____

to   _____   over   _____

for   _____   in front   _____

at   _____   after   _____

with   _____   of / from _____

on   _____   behind   _____

before   _____   beside   _____

                                  without   _____

C. Translate into English.

C'est pour moi. _____

C'est dans la
poubelle. _____

C'est à l'école. _____

C'est chez Nicole. _____

C'est devant le
pupitre. _____

C'est sur la table. _____

C'est après l'école. _____

Il est avec moi. _____

C'est sous la chaise. _____

D. Draw the correct picture using arrows.

dans le réfrigérateur	sur la tête	sous la table

Unit Seven:
Alphabet

Alphabet

A. Introduction

The best way to introduce the alphabet is to find a CD with the alphabet song in French. It can also be downloaded from the internet.

Kids know this song and are amused by the differences from the English version. Even older kids don't seem to mind singing when it's in a different language.

Have the kids sing through a couple of times together with the CD.

One possible "ending" of the song is:

"Je connais mon alphabet.

C'est facile comme tu le sais."

Kids could practice and perform the song in small groups and add dance moves, or their own creative ideas.

B. Online Practice

The kids need to hear the French alphabet repeatedly to learn the correct pronunciation.

There are many online activities available on the internet for kids to hear the alphabet song in French.

There are also interactive games that help teach the identification of letters by their pronunciation.

C. More Practice

Obtain or create some ABC flashcards to show the class to practice identifying letters without singing the alphabet song. This is a good 2 minute filler activity to practice any time with the class.

D. Line-up!

Each student is assigned one letter from the alphabet.

Speaking only in French, students should line themselves up in alphabetical order.

The letters can then be reassigned and the game played over.

E. Back-writing.

The class is divided into 4 teams.

The teams line up facing the chalkboard.

A letter is written on the backs of the 4 students at the ends of the lines (away from the chalkboard).

When the teacher says "Go!" the 4 end students write the letter (without speaking) on the back of the team mate in front of them and so on up the line.

The person at the chalkboard then writes the letter down and says it in French. The team done first, and correctly, wins.

F. Air-Writing

The teacher "air writes" a letter to the class.

Students can call out the letter in French.

The teacher could "air write" a series of letters with students writing their guesses.
Students could then read out and check their answers.

G. Testing Comprehension

The alphabet needs to be recited to know if students have good knowledge of it.

An oral portion of a French test could test alphabet knowledge.

Unit Eight: Holidays

Halloween

A. Vocabulary List

Halloween   _____

des bonbons   _____

un potiron   _____

un vampire   _____

un masque   _____

un déguisement   _____

le trente-et-un octobre   _____

un monstre   _____

une sorcière   _____

un squelette   _____

un fantôme   _____

une araignée   _____

un chat noir   _____

une chauve-souris   _____

un feu follet   _____

un cimetière   _____

une momie   _____

B. Translate into French.

It's Halloween! _____

October 31 _____

candy _____

a spider _____

Halloween _____

a black cat _____

a witch _____

a ghost _____

a skeleton _____

a costume _____

a pumpkin _____

a mask _____

a vampire _____

a monster _____

a bat _____

C. Halloween Word Scrambler

revisochusau _____   recoseri _____

welleahon _____   netsugideem _____

meatnof _____   parviem _____

telqueste _____   nosobnb _____

quames _____   gaineare _____

D. Halloween Word Search

```
E  R  E  I  C  R  O  S  V  Z  T  M
A  T  A  R  A  I  G  N  E  E  M  A
D  E  G  U  I  S  E  M  E  N  T  S
M  B  O  N  B  O  N  S  B  Y  H  Q
J  Y  D  R  I  O  N  T  A  H  C  U
E  R  T  S  N  O  M  P  Y  A  Z  E
S  I  R  U  O  S  E  V  U  A  H  C
D  K  P  O  T  I  R  O  N  O  M  K
E  T  T  E  L  E  U  Q  S  L  V  T
H  A  L  L  O  W  E  E  N  R  X  I
```

ARAIGNÉE	DÉGUISEMENT	POTIRON
BONBONS	HALLOWEEN	SORCIÈRE
CHAT NOIR	MASQUE	SQUELETTE
CHAUVE-SOURIS	MONSTRE	

Christmas

A. Vocabulary List

Noël   _____

Père Noël   _____

Joyeux Noël   _____

une carte de Noël   _____

l'arbre de Noël   _____

une chandelle   _____

un cadeau   _____

un jouet   _____

un ange   _____

une boule de neige   _____

un bonhomme de neige   _____

un renne   _____

un traîneau   _____

une canne à sucre   _____

un bas de Noël   _____

une étoile   _____

B. Translate into French.

It is a snowman.

_____

It's Christmas!

_____

toy   _____

snowman   _____

present   _____

snowball   _____

angel   _____

Santa Claus   _____

Merry Christmas   _____

Christmas tree   _____

Christmas card   _____

stocking   _____

C. Write a letter to Santa.

Write a letter to Santa Claus in French.

Use an online translation site or English-French dictionary if necessary.

Your letter may include:

- *a greeting*
- *an introduction*
- *a thank-you for last year's presents*
- *a request for certain presents this year*
- *a description of your behaviour this year*
- *a closing*

This letter should be done on the computer.

You may do an illustration or include pictures you find online.

D. French Christmas Carols

Research some French Christmas Carols on the internet.

Try to find one that is familiar to you in English.

Print it out and bring it to share with the class.

Include the English translation as well if it is available. Sometimes the English translation is not the way we usually sing it in English!

The class could try to sing the French carols together or you may form small groups to practice and then present a carol together.

Suggested Supplemental Activities

Supplemental Activities

The following activities are general activities that can be used to teach and practice several of the units and content areas.

To supplement the teaching of:
Colours/Body/Clothing/Descriptive Words

The teacher describes a student in the class or a famous person or character in French.

The students have to figure out who is being described.

They can write their answer on a scrap of paper when done.

OR

The teacher describes an object/person/thing and the class all draw their own picture of what is being described. A funny activity!

To supplement the teaching of:
Body/Animals/Clothing/Colours/Descriptive Words

Divide the class into two teams.

Draw two oval shapes on the board.

Call out "Dessinez mon nez!" and the two first students form each team run up and draw your nose in the oval provided.

Then call "Les yeux!" which is drawn by the next two students in line.

This can be done with a basic torso drawn instead of face ovals as well.

This could be adapted to do animal parts as well.

To supplement the teaching of:
All Vocabulary

A Spelling Bee is a great way to reinforce vocabulary.

Spelling Bees can also be done in teams for beginners. That way, they can confer on answers and have a better chance for success.

To supplement the teaching of:
All Vocabulary

Survivor Spelling Game

Make a list of vocabulary covered previously.

Have students stand up.

Call out a vocabulary word.

The first student begins by saying the word and then gives the first letter.

The second student gives the second letter, the third student the third letter, and so on until the word is spelled correctly.

If someone makes an error they must sit down and the word is started over again until it is spelled correctly.

The final student must then pronounce the word correctly and give a definition in order to stay standing.

To supplement the teaching of:
All Vocabulary

Students stand in a circle around the teacher.

The teacher tosses a ball to a student and asks a question or gives an "order" in French, e.g. "Saute!" or "Say a colour!"

The student responds and throws the ball back to the teacher.

The teacher throws the ball to a different student.

This activity can be made very easy or difficult depending on the questions.

To supplement the teaching of:
Vocabulary and Grammar

Listening (Song Puzzle)

For this activity, you need the lyrics of a song in French.
You will need to copy the lyrics for each student or pair of students.

Cut the lines of the song.
The students try to put the lines of the song in order as they listen.

You can play the song as many times as necessary.

To supplement the teaching of:
Vocabulary and Grammar

Video Scavenger Hunt

Choose a kids movie, record some TV commercials, or record a story from a French newscast.

Compile a list of things for them to find out by watching the video clip.

Some ideas are facts, figures, and numbers of particular words.

Let the kids work in teams and show the video several times.

To supplement the teaching of:
Sentences and Grammar

Whispering Game

Divide the class into two teams.

Line up the players.

The teacher whispers a message in French to the first player in each line then says "Go!"

Each player whispers the message to the next player until the last player gets the message.

The team that can say the message correctly first receives a point.

Rotate the lines and keep playing.

Answer Key

Unit One Check-Up

Part A L ; hot

Q ; night

G ; spring

A ; Thursday

K ; snow

P ; winter

C ; week

B ; Sunday

E ; hour

J ; weather

H ; Saturday

M ; Tuesday

R ; cold

D ; sun

O ; first

F ; August

I ; February

Part B 1. What is the date?

2. It is sunny.

3. It is windy.

Part C 1. Il neige.

2. Cést jeudi, le 10 novembre.

Unit Two Check-Up

Part A N ; fifteen

D ; yellow

J ; fat

A ; grey

L ; fast

P ; beautiful

I ; forty

K ; black

M ; eleven

R ; five

E ; old

O ; young

Q ; many

F ; twenty

G ; white

B ; pink

H ; thirteen

C ; sixty

Part B 1. It's black.

2. It's big.

Part C 1. Combien?

2. C'est vert clair.

Part D

50	12
100	17
8	70
11	80
15	2

112

Unit Three Check-Up

Part A   H ; bird

F ; computer

G ; pen

K ; bread

L ; bed

C ; cheese

O ; desk

A ; notebook

E ; chair

N ; dog

P ; food

B ; breakfast

J ; window

M ; fish

D ; bedroom

I ; cow

Part B   1. It's a house.

2. It's a flower.

Part C   1. C'est un crayon.

2. C'est un chat.

Part D   le paper   l'école

l'ordinateur   la pomme

Unit Four Check-Up

Part A   M ; She is calm.

A ; We have

C ; She is angry.

H ; You are sad.

B ; They are

L ; He is tired.

I ; I am

E ; He sings.

D ; I am happy.

J ; They are scared.

K ; She falls

F ; He talks.

G ; He eats.

Part B   He's excited.

I'm hungry.

He walks to school.

He likes the sun.

She thinks.

He reads the book.

Part C   Elle mange.

Il chante

Je suis.

Il est.

J'ai

Unit Five Check-Up

Part A   F ; underwear

                H ; arm

                B ; teeth

                G ; eyes

                J ; shoes

                K ; hand

                L ; hair

                D ; sister

                N ; boy

                A ; ears

                I ; shirt

                M ; foot

                C ; hat

                E ; socks

Part B   1. It's a girl.

                2. It's a hat.

Part C   eyes   glasses   pants

                mouth   boots   girl

www.ingramcontent.com/pod-product-compliance
Lightning Source LLC
Chambersburg PA
CBHW062048090426
42740CB00016B/3054